Environmental Science:
A Practical Manual

Environmental Science:
A Practical Manual

Edited by

G. Swarajya Lakshmi

P. Prabhu Prasadini

Ramesh Thatikunta

and

V.N.L.V. Tayaru

Acharya N.G.Ranga Agricultural University
Dept. of Bioresources Management
Programme on Environmental Science & Technology
College of Agriculture, Rajendranagar
Hyderabad - 500 030

BSP BS Publications

An Imprint of BSP Books Pvt. Ltd.
4-4-309/316, Giriraj Lane,
Sultan Bazar, Hyderabad - 500 095

Environmental Science: A Practical Manual
***by* G. Swarajya Lakshmi, P. Prabhu Prasadini and Ramesh Thatikunta**

Third Reprint 2024

Published by:

BSP BS Publications
An Imprint of BSP Books Pvt. Ltd.
4-4-309/316, Giriraj Lane, Sultan Bazar,
Hyderabad - 500 095
Phone: 040 - 23445688
e-mail: info@bspbooks.net
website: www.bspbooks.net

Printed at
Repro India Limited.

Price: Rs. 225.00
ISBN: 978-81-7800-228-6 (Paperback)

Grams: "AGRIVARSITY"
5Phones: 24015011 (7 lines) FAX : 091-040-2015197
24015161 (3 lines) Cell : 9989633306
E-mail: deanagri@hotmail.com

ACHARYA N.G. RANGA AGRICULTURAL UNIVERSITY

ADMINISTRATIVE OFFICE: RAJENDRANGAR, HYDERABAD – 500 030

Dr. T. YELLAMANDA REDDY
Dean of Agriculture

Foreword

For betterment of mankind, since time immemorial the natural resources which include soil, water and air have been utilized. Towards meeting the food and nutritional requirement of biota, crops have been under cultivation. Now with the increase in population, pressure is exerted on the natural resources with a result of their over exploitation. At times, the overuse of resources has also resulted in their loss or pollution. The nature however has not been able to recoup and keep pace with their utility. Especially, in urban and peri-urban areas, the water requirements of crops are met from a mix of river water, ground water and waste water. These waters pose threat to environment, health of crops and human beings owing to the presence of excess amounts of nutrients, microbes and heavy metals that result in biomagnifications in human food chain. Besides, the decreased amount of water availability for various purposes has resulted in a change in cropping pattern from agricultural / horticultural crops cultivation to growing of fodders to construction of industries and residential houses. But for these reasons, for sustainable livelihoods a time has come for continuous evaluation, monitoring and taking initiative for restoration and conservation of the natural resources.

The present practical manual for undergraduate students highlights the exercises that reveal the technologies available for quantification of pollutants which chiefly cause pollution. Visits to local polluted sites, observations and remedial measures, *In situ* and *ex situ* conservation practices are separately dealt to invoke and open up the young minds to take up action. As I understand, the manual is helpful for undergraduate students in tandem with the environmental issues copping up and the technologies which in my view would accrue benefits to mankind in future by way of sustainable living.

The practical manual written by Dr G Swarajya Lakshmi and her group is highly useful to the students of Environmental Science. The efforts taken by the teachers are highly appreciated.

12/3/10

(T. Yellamanda Reddy)

Preface

Mother earth has been considered as a safe place to live in and eke a living. Over time, again concerns have been expressed on the differences that exist between the standards of living and quality of life of people in rural, peri-urban and urban areas. Livelihood of the citizens depended on the monsoon. Vagaries in monsoon however, has very frequently resulted in either flood or drought situation and the communities were not able to cope with the required wherewithal's. Earth's capacity to replenish the natural resources now started to lag behind the requirement over time. Elite who only form a small fraction of the population having the means showed a sustainable living. In the same fashion, developed countries which have been exploiting the natural resources excessively used them for their needs and grew richer. Their concerns for environmental quality and actions taken up towards maintaining the cleaner environment, were realized much later. In contrast, the mitigation measures taken up in developing countries have only been limited to those distressed periods. No law has been in place to look into the actual needs of the large effected population. Lack of proper delivery system compounded the problem of transfer of goods and services. Hence, India today is facing the twin problem of growing population, meeting the need for food / nutritional requirement and cleaner environment, which has put up enormous pressure on the available resources.

To produce more food, chemical fertilizers, pesticides and various other inputs are being used in excess and in an indiscriminate manner. Consequent to this, the residues of these chemicals have been piling up in ecosystems and further degrading them. Differences in the consumption patterns by the affluent sections *vis a vis* less fortunate people is leading to the concept of equitable distribution of resources and the need for sustainable use of resources. Towards population control, family planning measures and simultaneous education of masses are some of the measures taken up. Sustainable practices, such as the best practices, which have gained importance in this direction are the use of organic inputs, integrated nutrient management, protecting soil health, water conservation, integrated pest management, restoration of aquatic bodies, conservation of forests, protecting the indigenous tribes and sharing the benefits with the masses.

Keeping in view the above developments and to safeguard the natural resources, it has become primarily important to realize their importance and develop indices to quantify the multifaceted aspects of environmental degradation. The present practical manual aims in the direction and lays emphasis on conservation, preservation and restoration of available natural resources. The authors hope that the manual meets the requirements of the clientele *i.e.,* the undergraduate students and also meets the standards set by the fourths Deans committee on the syllabus revision as laid out by the UGC of our country.

- Authors

CERTIFICATE

Certified that this is a bonafide record of work done by ____, for the course Environmental Science.

COURSE TEACHER

Contents

EXPERIMENT 1

Collection, Processing and Storage of Effluent Samples

Introduction

Water pollution is mainly caused by two sources such as point and non-point. This depends on how the pollution enters the water. Point sources are sources of pollution situated at one location, often a specific outlet (discharge) pipe. Factories and wastewater treatment plants usually have discharge pipes leading directly to the water body. Pollution from non-point sources does not come from one specific location; instead, it comes from many small sources in a large area. It is usually caused by water which flows over land to a river, a lake for example, rain water and irrigation water. As this water passes over the ground, it picks up pollutants and carries them into local waters. Non-point source of pollution can also result from pollution in the air that falls into the water or on the ground. In general, non-point sources are more difficult to identify.

Aim

To collect a portion of material small enough in volume to be transported conveniently and handled in the laboratory still accurately representing the material being sampled.

Apparatus

Sample containers

There are two basic choices in containers *viz*., glass or plastic. In both the cases a tightly fitting screw cap top is essential. Borosilicate glass is the best. Adsorption or ion exchange on the glass surface invalidates the use of glass bottles for storage of water in which heavy metals are to be estimated. As compared to glass bottles, plastic bottles are inexpensive and less fragile and less ion exchange problem. Among the plastics, high density linear polythene may be used. Containers made of fluorinated polymers such as polytetrafluoroethylene (TFE) can be preferred for sampling organics.

Bottle cleaning

Plastic bottles including teflon may contain impurities which will result in sample contamination. The method of cleaning depends on the use to which the bottles will be put. At the very least, however, most inorganic analysis applications require that the container be with detergent rinsed thoroughly with tap water and finally with distilled or de-ionized water. A non-ionic detergent used in hot water is the best when heavy metals are to be analyzed. In such cases acid soaking (1:1 HNO_3 or HCl) followed by detergent wash is essential.

Sampling Procedure

Number of samples depends on the size of selected site and number of sampling stations. Typically an area is divided into a series of blocks and sampling sites are identified either in the centre of each unit or at the intersection of each unit. Depending on the size of the project and the predicted distribution of the parameters or constituents of interest, the intensity of sampling can be selected. In projects, dealing with environmental pollution of a small area, sampling stations usually need to be located very close, particularly in areas with many contaminant sources. In an environmental survey, the goal is to check the extent of pollution and the presence and abundance of specific pollutants. Samples taken within a grid block is representative of the pollution for the area surrounding the sampling point.

As there are random variations in both analytical procedures as well as occurrence of a constituent at a point, a single sample may be insufficient. First assess the overall standard deviation; approximately 20-30 samples have to be taken, and for most physical and chemical analyses, a 2L sample is sufficient.

Size of the sampling area

The number and distance between sampling stations also depend on the physical size of the study area and how large each sample has to represent. In addition, the density of sampling stations is determined by the variability or gradients in the processes, which control the distribution of the investigated parameter.

Types of Samples

Grab or catch sample: The sample collected at a particular time and place which represent only the composition at that time and place. When a source is known to be constant in composition over a considerable period of time, then such a source may be represented well by single grab sample.

When a source is known to vary with time, grab samples collected at suitable intervals and analyzed separately can document the extent, frequency, and duration of these variations. Choose sampling intervals on the basis of the expected frequency of changes, which may vary from as little as 5 min to as long as 1 h or more. Seasonal variations in natural systems may necessitate sampling over months. When the source composition varies in space *i.e.,* from location to location rather than time, collect samples from appropriate locations that will meet the objectives of the study (e.g., upstream and downstream from a point source *etc.,*). Take every possible precaution to obtain a representative sample.

Composite sample: It refers to the mixture of grab samples collected at the same sampling point at different times. A composite sample representing a 24 hours period is considered standard for most determinations. For determining components or characteristics subject to significant unavoidable changes on storage, composite samples should not be used.

Preservation and storage: Collect individual portions in a wide-mouth bottle every hour (in some cases every half hour or even every 5 min) and mix at the end of the sampling period or combine in a single bottle as collected. If preservatives are used, add them to the sample bottle initially so that all portions of the composite are preserved as soon as collected.

Integrated sample: For certain purposes, the information needed is provided best by analyzing the mixtures of grab samples collected from different points simultaneously or as nearly so as possible. Such mixtures sometimes are called integrated samples.

Sampling Methods

Manual sampling: Manual sampling involves minimal equipment but may be unduly costly and time-consuming for routine or large-scale sampling programs. It requires trained field technicians and is often necessary for regulatory and research investigations for which critical appraisal of field conditions and complex sample collection techniques are essential. Manually collect certain samples, such as waters containing oil and grease.

Automatic sampling: Automatic samplers can eliminate human errors in manual sampling, can reduce labour costs, may provide the means for more frequent sampling, and are used increasingly. Be sure that the automatic sampler does not contaminate the sample. For example, plastic components may be incompatible with certain organic compounds that are soluble in the plastic parts or that can be contaminated (e.g., from phthalate esters) by contact with them. If sample constituents are generally known, contact the manufacturer of an automatic sampler regarding potential incompatibility of plastic components. Program an automatic sampler in accordance with sampling needs. Carefully match pump speeds and tubing sizes to the type of sample to be taken.

Sorbent sampling: Use of solid sorbents, particularly membrane-type disks is becoming more frequent. These methods offer advantages of rapid, inexpensive sampling if the analytes of interest can be adsorbed and desorbed efficiently and the water matrix is free of particulates that plug the sorbent.

Field log Book

This should include purpose of sampling, location of sampling point, name and address of the field contact, producer of material being sampled and address (if different from location). Suspected sample composition including concentrations, number and volume of samples taken, description of sampling point and sampling method, date and time of collection, collector's identification number and sample distribution with transport particulars. Protect the log book and keep it in safe place.

Chain-of-custody record

Properly designed and executed chain-of-custody forms will ensure sample integrity from collection to data reporting. This includes the ability to trace possession and handling of the sample from the time of collection through analysis and final disposition. This process is referred to as "chain-of-custody" and is required to demonstrate sample control when the data are to be used for regulation or litigation. Where litigation is not involved, chain-of-custody procedures are useful for routine control of samples. A sample is considered to be under a person's custody if it is in the individual's physical possession, in the individual's sight, secured and tamper-proofed by that individual, or secured in an area restricted to authorized personnel.

This should accompany each sample or groups of samples. The record includes sample number, signature of the collector, date, time, and address of collection, samples type, signatures or persons involved in the chain of possession and inclusive of the dates of possession.

Preservation of Samples

After examining the information accompanying the sample and verification regarding any tampering collection, the sample should be stored in a secured place. Certain cations (Al, Cd, Cr, Cu, Fe, Pb, Mn, Ag and Zn) are subject to loss by adsorption on or ion exchange with the walls of glass containers. These are best collected in a separate clean bottle and acidified with HNO_3 to a pH below 2.0 to minimize precipitation and adsorption to container walls. The sample should be stored in a secured place. Parameters which need immediate estimation include parameters like pH, free CO_2, alkalinity, dissolved oxygen and sulphide. For physical and chemical analysis some holding time for sample is permissible. Most of the samples may be stored at 4°C. Chemical preservatives should be used only when they are shown not to interfere with the analysis being made (Table in page 6).

Table Summary of special sampling or handling requirements.

S No.	Test to be conducted	container	Minimum sample size - ml	Preservation procedure	Maximum storage time
1	Acidity	P,G(B)[+]	100	Refrigerated*	24 hours
2	Alkalinity	P,G	200	Refrigerated	24 hours
3	BOD	P,G	1000	Refrigerated	6 / 48 hours
4	COD	P,G	100	Analyze as soon as possible or add H_2SO_4 to bring pH to < 2	7 days / 28 days
5	Chlorine residue	P,G**	500	Refrigerated and to be analyzed immediately	0.5 hours
6	Chlorophyll	P,G	500	30 days in dark	30 days
7	Hardness	P,G	100	Add HNO_3 to bring pH to < 2	6 months
8	Metals	P(A),G(A)***	--	For dissolved metals filter immediately and HNO_3 to bring pH to < 2	6 months
9	pH	P,G	--	Analyze immediately	0.5 hours
10	Turbidity	P,G	--	Analyze same day	24 hours
11	Solids	P,G	--	Refrigerated	7 days
12	Dissolved oxygen	G, BOD bottle	300	Analyze immediately	0.5 hours

* Refrigerated means sample is stored at 4°C in dark

** P = Plastic, G = Glass

*** P (A), G (A) = rinsed with 1+1 HNO_3

[+] G (B) =glass, borosilicate

G (S) = glass rinsed with organic solvents

Sample seals and labels

Gummed paper labels of tags are generally adequate. Labels should include name of the collector, date, hour, exact location, water temperature, water level, post sampling handling and steam flow. Labels should be filled before or at the time of sampling with water proof ink.

Precautions in Collection of Water Samples

- Hot water samples collected under pressure should be cooled while they are still under pressure.
- Well water should be pumped sufficiently to ensure that sample collected represents ground water source.
- Pipe lines should be sufficiently flushed before collecting from distribution systems.
- Surface scum should be avoided while sampling.
- Samples should be collected beneath the surface in quiescent areas.
- Excessive turbulence causes potential loss of volatile constituents and toxic vapours, hence areas of excessive turbulence are to be avoided.

Sample Delivery to the Laboratory

This should be done as soon as possible to the sample custodian.

General precautions

- Samples should be obtained and handled in such a way that it does not deteriorate or become contaminated before it reaches the laboratory
- In case of collection of waste water sampling, bottle used is to be rinsed two or three times with the sampling water itself unless otherwise the bottle contains a preservative of dechlorinating agent
- In case of organic determinations sample should be filled full in the bottle
- Samples if shipped, an air space of about one percent is to be left
- Adequate care needs to be taken when processing samples, for trace contaminants
- Depending on local conditions of water bodies, depth and frequency of the samples have to be determined.

EXPERIMENT 2

Determination of Chemical Oxygen Demand in Waste Water Sample

Introduction

Chemical oxygen demand (COD) is the oxygen requirement of a sample for oxidation of organic and inorganic matter under specified conditions corrected for the influence of chlorides. The major advantage of the COD test is, the short time required to carry out rather than the longer 5 days procedure for BOD. This test is recommended as a supplement to BOD test.

In COD test, the sample is subjected to chemical oxidation included by chemical reagents and it is an artificial oxidation by which both biologically oxidisable and biologically inert organic matter are oxidized.

Aim

To estimate the amount of organic matter and in turn COD of the waste water sample using a strong chemical oxidant namely potassium dichromate ($K_2Cr_2O_7$)

Apparatus

COD reflux unit consisting flat bottom flask with ground glass mouth (250 ml) with leibig (straight tube, single surface) condenser (30 cm), hot water bath or heating mantle, burette and pipette

Observations

Standardization of ferrous ammonium sulphate:

S. No	Volume of potassium dichromate taken	Ferrous ammonium sulphate rundown		Titre value (Final – Initial) ml
		Burette reading (Initial)	Burette reading (Final)	
1.	10 ml			
2.	10 ml			

Calculations:

$V_1N_1 = V_2N_2$ Where

V_1, V_2 = volume of $K_2Cr_2O_7$ & $[Fe(NH_4)_2(SO_4)_2]$ run down, respectively

N_1, N_2 = Normality of $K_2Cr_2O_7$ (0.25N) & $[Fe(NH_4)_2(SO_4)_2]$, respectively

Observations: for actual experiment

S. No	Volume of Sample taken	Ferrous ammonium sulphate rundown		Titre value (Final – Initial) ml (T)
		Burette reading (Initial)	Burette reading (Final)	
1	10 ml			
2	10 ml			
3				
4				

S. No	Volume of Blank taken	Ferrous ammonium sulphate rundown		Titre value (Final – Initial) ml (B)
		Burette reading (Initial)	Burette reading (Final)	
1	10 ml			
2	10 ml			
3				

Reagents

1. Standard potassium dichromate ($K_2Cr_2O_7$) 0.25N: weigh 12.258 g of $K_2Cr_2O_7$ and dissolve in distilled water and make up the volume to 1000 ml with distilled water in a volumetric flask .
2. $HgSO_4$ and $AgSO_4$ crystals
3. Concentrated H_2SO_4
4. Ferroin indicator: Dissolve 0.695 g of ferrous sulphate ($FeSO_4,7H_2O$) and 1.485 g of 1:10 phenonthroline in distilled water and make up the volume to 100 ml
5. Standard ferrous ammonium sulphate [Fe $(NH_4)_2$ $(SO_4)_2$]. (0.25N): Dissolve 39.29 g of ferrous ammonium sulphate in distilled water and add 20 ml of conc. H_2SO_4 and make up the volume to 1000 ml with distilled water. Standardize it against 0.25N potassium dichromate as follows: Pipette out 10 ml of 0.25N potassium dichromate solution into a 250 ml conical flask. Dilute to 100 ml and add 20 ml of conc. sulphuric acid and cool to room temperature. Add 2 to 5 drops of ferroin indicator and titrate with ferrous ammonium sulphate (FAS) solution. The end point is the colour change from bluish green to reddish brown. The exact normality of FAS is calculated by using the formula

$$V_1N_1 = V_2N_2$$

Principle

The organic matter present in the given sample of wastewater is oxidized to CO_2 and H_2O by refluxation with a known excess amount of chromic acid ($K_2Cr_2O_7 + H_2SO_4$) by using heat of dilution of H_2SO_4. The excess $K_2Cr_2O_7$ which is left over after oxidation is titrated with standard ferrous ammon sulphate by using ferroin as indicator till bluish green colour changes to reddish brown colour. Simultaneously blank is conducted to know the actual amount of $K_2Cr_2O_7$ consumed for oxidation which is proportional to the oxygen required to oxidize the organic matter.

Calculations

1000 ml of 1N FAS = 8 gm of O_2

$$1000 \text{ ml of } 0.25\text{N FAS} = \frac{0.25}{1} \times 8\text{gm of } O_2$$

Titre value with sample = T ml

Titre value without sample (blank) = B ml

Amount of 0.25N FAS actually utilized for oxidation = (B – T) = x ml

$$\text{x ml of } 0.25\text{N FAS} = \frac{x}{1000} \times \frac{0.25}{1} \times 8 \text{ gm } O_2$$

Volume of sample taken (V) = 10 ml

$$\therefore \quad 10 \text{ ml of sample} = \frac{x}{1000} \times \frac{0.25}{1} \times 8 \text{ gm } O_2$$

$$\text{Then } 1000 \text{ ml of sample} = \frac{1000}{10} \times \frac{x}{1000} \times \frac{0.25}{1} \times 8 \text{ gm of } O_2$$

$$= \frac{x}{10} \times 0.25 \times 8\text{gm of } O_2$$

$$\therefore \quad \text{COD in (mg L}^{-1}) == \frac{x}{10} \times 0.25 \times 8 \times 1000$$

Procedure

- Pipette 20 ml of the sample into the flask of reflux unit.
- Add 10 ml of 0.25N $K_2Cr_2O_7$ through pipette.
- Add a pinch of each silver sulphate and mercuric sulphate and 30 ml of concentrated H_2SO_4.
- Attach liebig condenser to the mouth of flask and heat the flask on a hot water bath or heating mantle for at least 2 hours to reflux the contents.
- Cool the flask, detach from unit and dilute the contents to about 150 ml by adding distilled water.
- Add 2-3 drops of ferroin indicator and titrate the contents of the flask with 0.25N ferrous ammonium sulphate solution till bluish green colour changes to reddish brown.
- Run simultaneously a blank without sample, with distilled water in a similar manner.

Interference ions removal

The interference caused by chlorides can be eliminated by the addition of mercuric sulpate (Hg SO_4) to the sample prior to the addition of other reagents. Addition of silver sulphate to concentrated H_2SO_4 promotes the oxidation of straight chain aliphatic and aromatic compounds like acetic acid, amino acids *etc* as a catalyst.

Nitrates can be eliminated by the addition of 10 mg of sulphonic acid. For complete oxidation of organic matter, it is necessary to see that equal volumes of H_2SO_4 and the sample plus dichromate are taken.

Results and Inference:

EXPERIMENT 3

Determination of Dissolved Oxygen in Waste Water sample

Introduction

Dissolved oxygen analysis measures the amount of gaseous oxygen dissolved in an aqueous solution. Oxygen gets into water by diffusion form the surrounding air, by aeration and as a by-product of photosynthesis. Adequate dissolved oxygen is necessary for good quality of water. Natural stream purification processes require adequate oxygen levels in order to provide for aerobic life forms. As dissolved oxygen levels in water drop below 5.0 mg/l, aquatic life is put under stress. Oxygen levels that remain below 1-2 mg/l for few hours can result in large fish kills.

Aim

To determine the amount of dissolved oxygen present in the given waste water sample by Winkler's method.

Apparatus

BOD bottles (100-300 ml), conical flask, 25 ml burette and 10 ml pipette

Reagents

1. *Manganous sulphate solution:* dissolve 96 g of manganous sulphate ($MnSO_4.4H_2O$) in 200 ml of previously boiled distilled water and filter the same if solution is not clear.
2. *Alkal-iodide-azide solution:* Dissolve 37.5 g of potassium iodide and 175g of potassium hydroxide in 250 ml of previously boiled distilled water. Dissolve 2.5 g sodium azide in 10 ml distilled water in a separate beaker. Then pour this azide solution to the alkali-iodide solution and mix well.
3. *Sodium thiosulphate solution (0.1N):* Dissolve 24.82 g of sodium thiosulphate in previously boiled and cooled distilled water and make up the volume to 1 litre with distilled water to this add a pellet of sodium hydroxide as a preservative and preserve the solution in colored bottle.

Observations: Standardization of sodium thiosulphate

S. No	Volume of potassium dichromate taken	Sodium thio sulphate run down		Titre value (ml) (Final-Initial)
		Burette reading (Initial)	Burette reading (Final)	
1	10 ml			
2	10 ml			

Calculations

$$V_1N_1 = V_2N_2$$

where

V_1 = volume of potassium dichromate

N_1 = Normality of potassium dichromate

V_2 = Volume of sodium thiosulphate run down

N_2 = Normality of sodium thiosulphate

$$N_2 = \frac{V_1N_1}{V_2}$$

Observations: actual experiment

S. No	Volume of Sample taken	Sodium thio sulphate rundown		titre value (ml) (Final – Initial)
		Burette reading (Initial)	Burette reading (Final)	
1	100 ml			
2	100 ml			

4. Starch indicator: dissolve 1 g of starch in 100 ml of warm distilled water and add few drops of toluene or formaldehyde as preservative.
5. Concentrated sulphuric acid: Specific gravity 1.84.
6. ***Standardization of sodium thiosulphate using standard potassium dichromate***: Dissolve 1.23 g potassium dichromate (previously dried at 103^0C for 1 hr) in distilled water and make up to 250 ml in a volumetric flask with distilled water. This is exactly 0.1N solution. Pipette 10 ml of 0.1N potassium dichromate into a conical flask and add 1 drop of starch indicator. Titrate the above solution with sodium thiosulphate. End point is from blue to colourless. Calculate the normality of sodium thiosulphate solution by using the formula $V_1N_1=V_2N_2$

Principle

The "Winkler's" method is followed to estimate the DO value. This method is based on the fact that, when manganous sulphate is added to the sample containing alkaline potassium iodide, manganous hydroxide is formed, which is oxidized by dissolved oxygen of the sample to basic manganic oxide. In the presence of iodine and on subsequent acidification the basic manganic oxide revert to the divalent state and liberate iodine equivalent to that of dissolved oxygen originally present in the sample. The liberated iodine is titrated with standard solution of sodium thiosulphate using starch as an indicator.

Chemical reactions

$MnSO_4 + 2KOH \rightarrow Mn(OH)_2 + K_2SO_4$ (white ppt)

$2Mn(OH)_2 + O_2 \longrightarrow 2MnO(OH)_2$ (Basic manganic oxide)

(Dissolved oxygen)

$MnO(OH)_2 + 2H_2SO_4 \rightarrow Mn(SO_4)_2 + 3H_2O$

(manganic sulphate)

$Mn(SO_4)_2 + 2KI \rightarrow MnSO_4 + K_2SO_4 + I_2$

$2Na_2S_2O_3 + I_2 \rightarrow Na_2S_4O_6 + 2NaI$

Calculations

1000 ml of 1N $Na_2S_2O_3$ = 8 gm of O_2

1000 ml of 0.025N $Na_2S_2O_3 = \frac{0.025}{1} \times 8$ gm of O_2

Titre value = x ml

$\therefore$ x ml of 0.025N $Na_2S_2O_2 = \frac{x}{1000} \times \frac{0.025}{1} \times 8$ gm of O_2

Volume (V) of sample taken = 100 ml

Then 100 ml of sample contain $\frac{x}{1000} \times \frac{0.025}{1} \times 8$ gm of O_2

Then 1000 ml (1 lt) of sample contains $\frac{x}{1000} \times \frac{0.025}{1} \times 8 \times \frac{1000}{100}$ gm of O_2

Do in mg $L^{-1} = \frac{x}{100} \times 0.025 \times 8 \times 1000$

Classification

DO	Condition
5-6 ppm	sufficient for most species
< 3 ppm	stressful to most aquatic species
< 2 ppm	fatal to most species
2 to 6.5 ppm	Hypoxia (low dissolved oxygen level in water)
15 mg/lit	High DO (freezing)
below 0.5 ppm	Anoxia (the absence of oxygen)

Procedure

- Pipette out 100 ml of sample into a glass stoppered BOD bottle.
- Add 1 ml each of manganous sulphate and alkali-iodide-azide solution using separate pipettes (if the sample volume exceeds 200 ml, add 2 ml each of the reagent)
- Stopper the bottle without any entrapped air and shake well by inverting the bottle at least for about 1 minuite
- Brown precipitate formed is allowed to settle down. Sample at this stage can be stored for few days if required
- Add 2 ml of conc. H_2SO_4 and shake well to dissolve the precipitate formed.
- Transfer the whole content or known part into a conical flask and titrate the contents with standard sodium thiosulphate solution.
- Add 2 ml of starch solution when the colour of the contents turn to straw yellow.
- Now the contents change to blue colour.
- Continue the titration till the disappreance of blue colour that is to colourless. Note down the titre value.

Results and Inference:

EXPERIMENT 4

Determination of Total Dissolved Solids in Waste Water Sample

Introduction

Dissolved solids or total dissolved solids (TDS) denote the mineral content in water in dissolved form. This may also include organic substances as in the case of polluted waters, and may also contribute to the total dissolved load. Dissolved solids do not contain any gas or colloids. However, determination of the dissolved solids does not give a clear picture of kind of pollution. Concentration of dissolved solids is an important parameter in drinking water and other water quality standards.

High concentration of dissolved solids, about 3000 mg L^{-1} produce distress in livestock and not fit for use in industry. Also, use of water with high amounts of dissolved solids lead to scaling of boilers, corrosion resulting in degraded quality of the product.

Aim

To find out the amount of total dissolved solids present in the given waste water sample, gravimetrically.

Apparatus

Porcelain dish, desiccator, water bath, filter paper and funnel

Principle: A known volume of water is evaporated to dryness and the quantity of soluble salts present is estimated gravimetrically

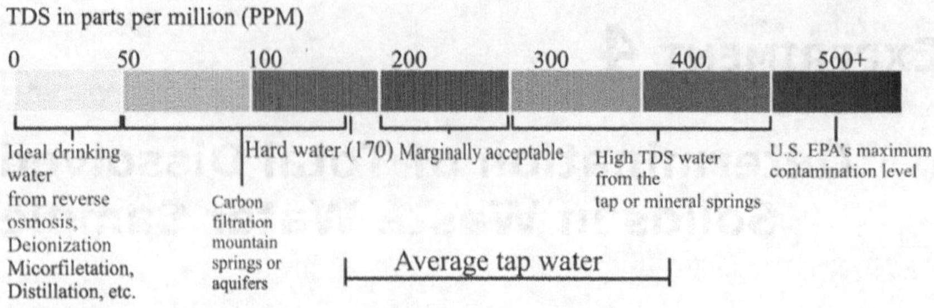

Observations

Initial weight of dish = W_1 gm

Volume of sample taken = 100 ml

Weight of china dish after evaporation of sample = W_2 gm

Calculations

Weight of total dissolved solids = Weight of dish along with dry solid – Initial weight of dish

$$= (W2 - W1) \text{ gm}$$

Volume of sample taken = 100 ml

100 ml sample contains $(W_2 - W_1)$ gm of TDS

1000ml of sample contains $(W_2 - W_1) \times \frac{1000}{100} = W_2 - W_1 \times 10$ g of TDS

TDS mg/l = $(W_2 - W_1) \times 10 \times 1000$

Procedure

- Filter 100 ml of sample through whatman No.4 filter paper in a pre-weighed china dish (porcelain dish)
- Evaporate the sample on hot water bath until whole water is evaporated
- Note the weight of china dish after cooling it in a desiccator and calculate the total dissolve solids (TDS).

Results and Inference:

Note:

TDS also can be determined indirectly through electrical conductivity by multiplying the EC in micromhos per cm with 0.67.

EXPERIMENT 5

Analysis of Total Hardness of Waste Water Sample

Introduction

The determination of water hardness is a useful test which provides a measure of quality of water for households and industrial uses. Originally, water hardness is defined as the measure of the capacity of the water to precipitate soap. Hard water is due to metal ions (minerals) that are dissolved in the ground water. These minerals include calcium, magnesium, iron, sulphates and bicarbonates. Soap is precipitated by Ca and Mg of water. Other polyvalent cations are in complex forms with organic matter and their role is minimum. Therefore total hardness is the sum of Ca and Mg concentration, both expressed as $CaCO_3$ in mg L^{-1}. Mineral deposits are formed by ionic reactions resulting in the formation of an insoluble precipitate of calcium carbonate. When hard water is heated, $CaCO_3$ precipitates out; this then clogs pipes and industrial boilers. This leads to malfunction or damage and is expensive to remove. Total hardness of water is usually expressed as concentration of $CaCO_3$ (mg L^{-1}). By determination of Ca & Mg and by calculation, hardness of water is determined.

Hardness (mg equivalent of $CaCO_3$ L^{-1})

$$= 2.497\,[(\mathrm{Ca})\,(\mathrm{mg\ L^{-1}})] + 4.118\,[(\mathrm{Mg})\,(\mathrm{mg\ L^{-1}})]$$

A. Determination of calcium in waste water sample:

Aim

To determine the calcium present in the given waste water sample.

Apparatus

Burette, pipette, china dish and glass rod

Standardization of EDTA with $CaCO_3$ 0.01N

$V_1N_1 = V_2N_2$ where

V_1 = Volume of $CaCO_3$ = 10 ml

N_1 = Normality of $CaCO_3$ = 0.01N

V_2 = Volume of EDTA run down

N_2 = Normality of EDTA

$$\text{Normality of EDTA } (N_2) = \frac{10 \times 0.01}{V_2}$$

(a) Observations for Ca

S. No	Volume of sample taken	EDTA rundown		Titre value (ml) (Final – Initial)
		Burette reading (Initial)	Burette reading (Final)	
1	10 ml			
2	10 ml			
3	10 ml			

Calculations

1000 ml of 1N EDTA	=	20 g of Ca
1 ml of 1N EDTA	=	20 mg of Ca
1 ml of 0.01N EDTA	=	0.2 mg of Ca
Suppose Titre value	=	x ml
∴ x ml of 0.01N EDTA	=	x × 0.2mg of Ca
Volume of sample taken	=	10 ml
Then 10 ml of sample contains	=	x × 0.2 mg of Ca
Then 1000 ml of sample contains	=	$\frac{1000}{10} \times x \times 0.2$ mg of Ca = C

C = calcium in mg L^{-1} =

Reagents

1. Buffer solution (4N NaOH) dissolve 160 g pure sodium hydroxide in distilled water and make the volume to 1 litre with distilled water

2. Murexide: Also known as ammonium perpurate. Weigh 0.2 gm of ammonium perpurate and 40 gm of potassium sulphate. Mix both the regents thoroughly in a pestle and mortar and keep it as powder in a clean dark coloured bottle.

3. EDTA solution 0.01N: Dissolve 2 g of analytical reagent grade versenate (Ethylene diamine tetraacetate) in distilled water and make the volume to 1 litre with distilled water. Standardize the solution with 0.01N calcium solution.

4. Standard Calcium solution 0.01N: Weigh 0.5 g of anhydrous calcium carbonate and dissolve in 10 ml of 0.2N hydrochloric acid + 200 ml distilled water. Heat, till the solution boils and CO_2 is completely driven out. Then cool. Make up the solution to 1 lit. This solution has an equivalent of 1 ml = 1 mg of $CaCO_3$. Calcium solution is used to standardize the EDTA and to determine the exact strength of EDTA.

Principle

EDTA strongly complexes and forms chelates with a number of polyvalent cations such as those of Ca, Mg, Fe, Cu, Mn, Ni, Cd and Zn at different pH values. Based on this principle, a known volume of the waste water sample is titrated against standard EDTA solution in presence of sodium hydroxide buffer with ammonium perpurate (murexide) as indicator. The end point is a change of colour from orange red to purple at pH 12 when the whole of calcium forms a complex with EDTA.

Procedure

- Take 10 ml of water sample into a China dish with a pipette and add few ml of distilled water to increase the volume of solution.
- Add 1-2 ml of sodium buffer solution to the contents.
- Add a pinch of murexide indicator. Stir the contents well with glass rod. The contents turn to orange red colour.
- Titrate the contents of china dish with standard EDTA (0.01N) till orange red colour changes to purple or purplish violet.
- Note down the volume of EDTA run down.

Results and Inference:

(b) Observations for Ca + Mg

S. No	Volume of sample taken	EDTA rundown		Titre value (TV) ml (Final – Initial)
		Burette reading (Initial)	Burette reading (Final)	
1	10 ml			
2	10 ml			

Suppose TV for calcium + magnesium = a ml

TV for calcium = x ml

Then TV for magnesium = (a – x) ml = y ml

Calculations

1000ml of 1N EDTA	=	12 g of Mg
1 ml of 1N EDTA	=	12 mg of Mg
1 ml of 0.01N EDTA	=	0.12 mg of Mg
Titre value	=	y ml
y ml of 0.01N EDTA	=	$(0.12 \times y)$ mg of Mg
volume of sample taken	=	10 ml
$\therefore$ 10 ml of sample contains	=	$(y \times 0.12)$ mg of Mg
1 lt of sample contains	=	$1000 \times \frac{y \times 0.12}{10} = D$

D = magnesium in mg L^{-1} =

Total hardness of water (mg equivalent to $CaCO_3$ L^{-1})

= 2.497 {Ca (mg L^{-1}) + 4.118 {Mg (mg L^{-1})}.

= $(2.497 \times C) + (4.118 \times D)$

=

B. Determination of calcium + magnesium

Aim

To determine the amount of calcium + magnesium present in the given waste water sample.

Apparatus

Burette, pipette, china dish and glass rod

Reagents

1. Ammonium chloride and ammonium hydroxide buffer: Dissolve 67.5 g of ammonium chloride in 570 ml conc. ammonium hydroxide and make the volume to one litre with distilled water.
2. Eriochrome black T (EBT) indicator: Mix 0.5 g of the EBT dye and 4.5 g hydroxylamine hydrochloride and dissolve both in 100 ml of ethanol.
3. EDTA solution (0.01N): Dissolve 2 g of analytical reagent grade versenate (disodium ethylene amine tetra acetate dehydrate) in distilled water and make the volume to 1 litre with distilled water. Standardize the solution with 0.01N calcium solution.

Principle

A known volume of the given waste water sample is titrated against standard EDTA solution in presence of ammonium chloride and ammonium hydroxide buffer with eriochrome black T as indicator. At pH 10.0 Ca + Mg EDTA complex, forms which is shown by the end point from change of wine red colour to blue.

Procedure

- Take 10 ml of water sample into a china dish with a pipette and add few ml of distilled water to increase the volume of solution.
- Add 1-2 ml of ammonium chloride and ammonium hydroxide buffer solution to the contents.
- Add 2-3 drops of eriochrome black T. Stir the contents well with the help of glass rod. The contents turn to wine red colour.
- Titrate the contents of china dish with standard EDTA (0.01N) till wine red color changes to blue.
- Note down the volume of EDTA run down.

Results and Inference:

The degree of hardness of the water is classified in terms of its calcium carbonate concentration as follows:

Hardness rating	Concentration of Calcium Carbonate (mg/L)
Soft	0 to < 75
Medium hard	75 to < 150
Hard	150 to < 300
Very hard	300 and greater

Precautions

1. Interfering ions like Fe, Mn, Cu and Zn can be eliminated by converting them into their lower valency states by addition of hydroxylamine hydrochloride.
2. It is better if an untitrated sample after colour development is kept by the side of the samples being titrated to distinguish colour with change very precisely.
3. For Ca + Mg, the indicator, EDTA and buffer solution should be prepared fresh. Both these should be kept under refrigeration with tight cork.
4. EDTA on storage settles down at the bottom. Before use, either determine its normality again or prepare it fresh.
5. Suspended or colloidal organic matter may interfere with the end point. Sample could be evaporated and ignited in muffle furnace at 550^0 C. The residue so obtained could be dissolved in 20 ml HCl, neutralized to pH 7.0 with sodium hydroxide (1N), cooled and used for analysis.

Results and Inference:

EXPERIMENT 6

Analysis of Temporary Hardness of Waste Water Sample

Introduction

Sum of the carbonate (CO_3^{-2}) and bicarbonate (HCO_3^-) ions of calcium, magnesium and other bivalent constitutes the total alkalinity of the water as temporary hardness and raises its pH to more than 7.5. This is also known as carbonate hardness. This causes corrosion in the boilers and other metallic pipes. Hence its determination is also important for agricultural as well as industrial purposes. This can be removed by boiling.

Aim

To determine the temporary hardness in the given waste water sample

Apparatus

100 ml conical flask, 10 ml pipette and 25 ml burette

Reagents

1. Standard sulphuric acid (0.05N): Dilute 1.4 ml of concentrated H_2SO_4 (36N) to one litre with distilled water. This is standardized by using 0.05N sodium carbonate solution
2. Methyl orange indicator (0.5%): Dissolve 0.5 gm dry methyl orange powder in 100 ml of 95% alcohol.
3. Phenolphthalein indicator (0.25%): Dissolve 0.25 gm of pure phenolphthalein powder in 100 ml of 60% alcohol.

Observations

Volume of waste water sample taken = 10ml

Titre Value with phenolphthalein indicator

S. No.	Volume of sample ml	Burette reading		Titre value ml (Final – Initial)
		Initial	Final	

Titre Value with Methyl Orange indicator

S. No.	Volume of sample ml	Burette reading		Titre value ml (Final – Initial)
		Initial	Final	

Principle

Temporary hardness of waste water is determined by titrating against standard sulpuric acid using phenolphthalein and methyl orange as indicators. Phenolphthalein indicator enables the measurement of the alkalinity fraction contributed by the half of the carbonates *i.e,* the carbonates will be converted to bicarbonates which will be known by change of pink colour to colour less. Methyl orange indicator will help in neutralising the bicarbonate fractions of alkalinity *i.e.,* both converted and original bicarbonates which will be known by change in colour from straw yellow to rose red.

$$H_2SO_4 + CO_3^{2-} \longrightarrow 2HCO_3^- + SO_4^{2-}$$

$$2HCO_3^- + H_2SO_4 \longrightarrow 2H_2O + 2CO_2 + SO_4^{2-} \text{ (rose red)}$$

Procedure

- Pipette 10 ml of given water sample into a 100 ml conical flask
- Dilute it by adding about 25 ml of distilled water
- Add 2-3 drops of phenolphthalein indicator
- If the contents turn to pink colour, it indicates the presence of carbonates.
- If there is no pink colour, it indicates the absence of carbonates.
- If pink colour appears, titrate the contents against 0.05N H_2SO_4 till the disappreance of pink colour.
- Note down the titre value with phenolphthalein indicator
- Now add 2-3 drops of methyl orange indicator to the same colorless solution.
- The contents turn to straw yellow colour
- Continue the titration till straw yellow colour changes to rose red colour
- Note down the titre value with methyl orange indicator
- Repeat the titrations till two consecutive and concurrent readings are obtained

Calculations:

Carbonates

1 ml of 1N H_2SO_4 = 50 mg $CaCO_3$
Titre Value with phenolphthalein = y ml
Titre Value for carbonates = 2 y ml

$$2\text{ y ml of } 0.05\text{N } H_2SO_4 = 2y \times \frac{0.05}{1} \times 50 \text{ mg } CaCO_3$$

∴ 10 ml of sample contains = 2y × 0.05 × 50 mg $CaCo_3$

$$1000 \text{ ml contains} = \frac{1000}{10} \times 2y \times 0.05 \times 50 = A \text{ mg } CaCO_3$$

Carbonates Hardness = A mg $CaCO_3$ L^{-1} =

Bicarbonates

Titre Value with methyl organic indicator = x ml
1 ml of 1N H_2So_4 = 50 mg of CaCo3
Titre Value for bicarbonates = (x-y) ml
∴ (x-y) ml of 0.05N H_2So_4 = (x-y) × 0.05 × 50 mg of $CaCo_3$
Volume of sample taken = 10 ml
∴ 10ml of sample contains (x-y) × 0.05× 50 mg of $CaCo_3$
Bicarbonates hardness

$$= \text{T.V} \times \text{Normality of } H_2SO_4 \times 50 \times \frac{1000}{\text{volumen of sample}}$$

$$= (x\text{-}y) \times 0.05 \text{ x } 50 \times \frac{1000}{10} = B \text{ mg } CaCo_3\, L^{-1}$$

Bicarbonates hardness = B mg Ca CO_3 L^{-1} =

Temporary hardness = CO_3 hardness + HCO_3 hardness
= (A+B) mg $CaCO_3$ L^{-1}

Results and Inference:

Carbonates hardness (mg $CaCO_3$ L^{-1}) = ____________

Bicarbonates hardness (mg $CaCO_3$ L^{-1}) = ____________

Temporary hardness (mg $CaCO_3$ L^{-1}) = ______________

EXPERIMENT 7

Analysis of Waste Water/Sludge for Heavy Metals

Introduction

Now-a-days large amounts of untreated and sewage water is being discharged into surface water bodies without treatment. Farmers facing shortage of water and tend to utilize this water as a source of irrigation and in the process unknowingly accumulating the heavy metals in soils and thereby causing bioaccumulation and increasing the chances of biomagnifications. Living organisms require some heavy metals in trace amounts. Repeated application of waste water containing heavy metals may lead to accumulation of heavy metals to toxic levels in crops or animals or human beings which consume the crops.

Aim

To determine heavy metals in the given waste water sample using Atomic Absorption Spectrophotometer (AAS)

Apparatus

1000 ml volumetric flask, 100 ml Volumetric flasks, 100 ml conical flasks and funnels.

Reagents

Diethylene triamine penta acetic acid (DTPA) solution 0.005M: Transfer 1.965 g of DTPA, 13.3 ml of triethanol amine + 1.45 g of $CaCl_2 . 2H_2O$ into one litre volumetric flask. Add about 800 ml of double distilled water. Shake to dissolve the contents and adjust the pH to 7.3 with HCl and make the volume to 1 litre with double distilled water.

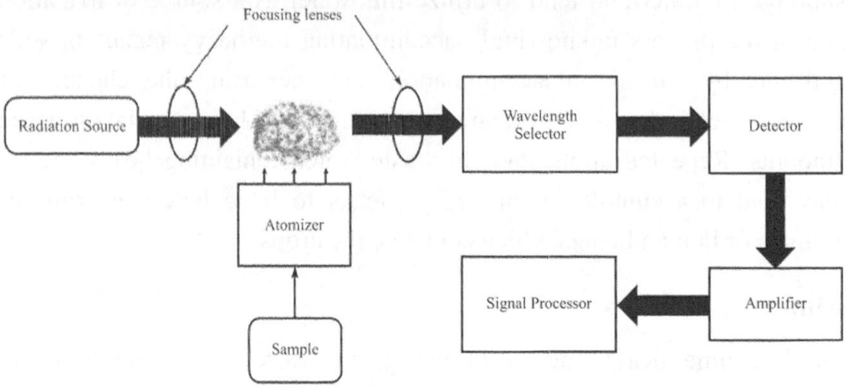
Focusing lenses
Radiation Source
Wavelength Selector
Detector
Atomizer
Sample
Signal Processor
Amplifier

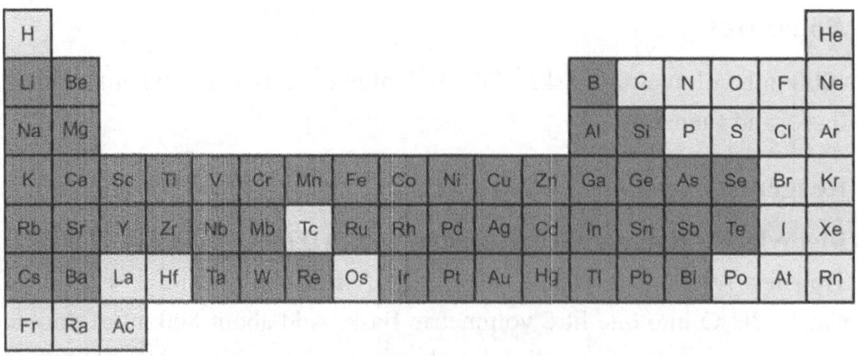
H He
Li Be B C N O F Ne
Na Mg Al Si P S Cl Ar
K Ca Sc Ti V Cr Mn Fe Co Ni Cu Zn Ga Ge As Se Br Kr
Rb Sr Y Zr Nb Mb Tc Ru Rh Pd Ag Cd In Sn Sb Te I Xe
Cs Ba La Hf Ta W Re Os Ir Pt Au Hg Tl Pb Bi Po At Rn
Fr Ra Ac

Working standards for Cr, Co, Ni, Cd, Pb: prepare 1000 ppm solutions from standard solution of the above elements and then transfer 0, 0.1, 0.25, 0.5, 1.0, 2.0, 4.0, 8.0 ml of 100 ppm solutions into 100 ml volumetric flasks and make up the final volume with double distilled water to obtain 0, 0.1, 0.25, 0.5, 1.0, 2.0, 4.0, 8.0 ppm standard solutions.

Principle

Atomic absorption spectrophotometer (AAS) is based on the principle that atoms of metallic element that normally remain in ground state under flame conditions absorb energy when subjected to radiations of specific wavelength. The absorption of radiation is proportional to the concentration of the atoms of the element.

The two most common oxidantful combinations used in AAS are air-acetylene and nitrous oxide-acetylene. Other flames that can be used are hydrogen and argon-hydrogen entrained air. The temperature ranges from 2125^0 to 2600^0 to 2800^0 C and used for the determination of elements, that form refractory oxides. Generally, flame is used for relatively higher concentration (ppm level) of heavy metals in soil and water, whereas, graphite furnace is used to quantify the trace amounts (ppb level). Use appropriate standards prepared in specific matrices and aspirate the samples into the AAS after instrument calibration. Follow the instrument parameters as given in the manual.

Components of AAS

1. A light source (that generates light at a wave length characteristic to a particular element)
2. A means of aspirating (atomizing an aqueous sample) by nebulizer or burner
3. A monochromator (separate light of the characteristic wavelength of an element from all other elements)
4. A light sensitive detector, usually a photo multiplier tube, (produces an electric signal proportional to the intensity of light.
5. A means of integrating 'reading' into digital output.

Calculation

ppm of heavy metal = (AAS reading in mg L^{-1} × dilution factor) / weight of the sample

Estimation in waste water

- Take the desired quantity of effluent water sample
- Add 1-2 ml of conc. HNO_3 and keep aside for 10-15 minutes
- Transfer the contents using whatman filter paper. Clear solution is used to note the absorbance in AAS.

Estimation in sludge

- Weigh one gram of air-dried sludge sample into acid washed 100 ml conical flask and add 20 ml of diacid (HNO_3: $HClO_4$ in 9:4 ratio) mixture.
- Add 40 ml of double distilled water.
- Digest the contents on a hot plate (at about 160°C) for 2 hours.
- Remove the conical flask from hot plate and cool the contents.
- Make up the contents to 100 ml with double distilled water.
- Filter the contents through whatman No.42 filter paper
- Take the reading of the filtrate in the AAS and by referring to the standard curve calculate the concentration of each metal in the sample

Precautions

1. The apparatus (glass/polyethylene/polypropylene) to be used for the analysis must be thoroughly washed with acidified water and then with double distilled water.
2. Shaking time, DTPA concentration, pH and temperature during shaking influence the amount of Zn, Cu, Mn and Fe extracted by DTPA.
3. The most suitable pH of extracting solution is 7.3
4. If the organic matter content is high, add few drops of n-Octanol to avoid frothing.

Results and Inference:

Digital Sound Level Meter

Model 407740

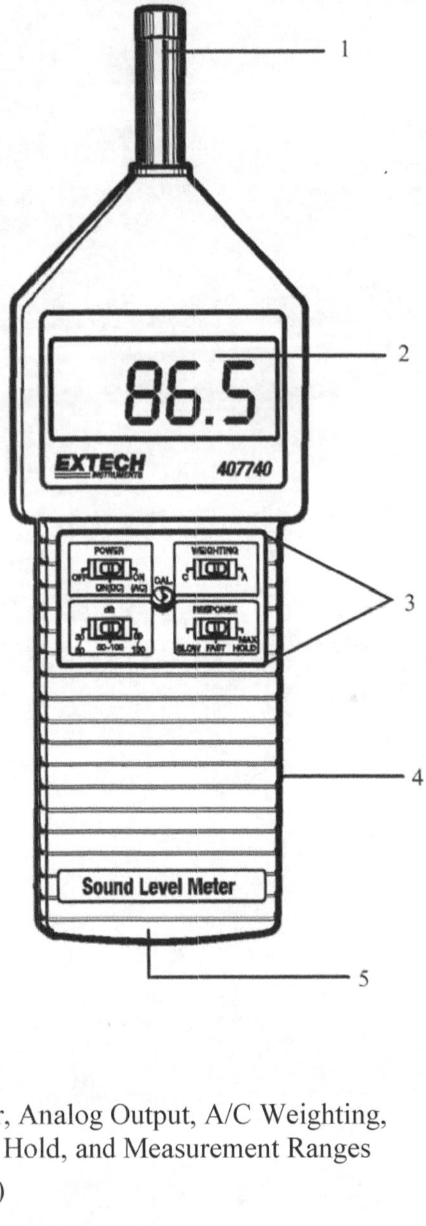

1. Microphone
2. LCD Display
3. Selector switches for power, Analog Output, A/C Weighting, Response Time, Maximum Hold, and Measurement Ranges
4. Battery Compartment (rear)
5. Analog output jack

EXPERIMENT 8

Determination of Sound Level by Using Sound Level Meter

Introduction

Noise is mainly defined as 'unpleasant' sound that causes discomfort to human ear. The word noise is defined as the 'wrong sound' in the 'wrong place' at 'wrong time'. The noise pollution problem is being increasing day by day and leads to several physiological disorders. The determination of noise and control of noise has become significant to avoid the noise pollution.

Aim

To determine the sound in various environments using a digital sound level meter.

Apparatus

Digital sound level meter (Extech 407740)

Principle: The sound is a form of energy producing longitudinal mechanical waves in matter including solid, liquid and gas (transmitting medium) by oscillation of atoms and molecules of matter. The receiver *i.e.,* microphone absorbs the energy from the transmitting medium and is determined on LCD in terms of decibels.

Some health hazards due to high noise are mentioned below.

Noise intensity (dB)	Health hazards
80	Annoying
90	Hearing damage (8 hr)
110	Stimulation of reception in skin
120	Pain threshold
130-135	Nausea, vomiting, dizziness
140	Pain in ear, prolonged exposure causing insanity
150	Significant change in pulse rate
180	Ear drum ruptures- major permanent damage

Observations

S.No.	Location	Sound in dB
1	In the class room	
2	Inside the plantation area	
3	Ringtone of cell	
4	At the bus stop (while bus is moving)	
5	At the bus stop	
6	Breathing (normal)	
7	Fan sound	
8	Claps	
9	Open area (without plants)	
10		
11		
12		

Procedure

- Turn the power switch to 'ON' to turn the meter on.
- Set the set switch to 'ON' (DC) to configure the analog out put to DC millivolts (1OmV/dB output).
- Use the WEIGHTING selector switch to select 'A' or 'C' frequency weighting. 'A' weighting is used for environmental measurements, OSH (Occupational Safety and Health) regulatory testing, law enforcement and work place design, 'C' weighting is suitable for operational maintenance and analysis of machinery motors, pump engines *etc.*
- Point the microphone towards the source where sound is to be measured.
- Select either fast or slow on 'RESPONSE' switch. Fast is selected to capture quick sound peaks.
- Select SLOW response with A weighting to the hearing conversation or OSHA related testing.
- Select the measuring range using the 'dB' selector switch. If the UPPER or LOWER indicator appears on the display while measuring sound levels, select a lower or higher range.
- The reading displayed is in dB of sound.
- Record maximum dB level selecting 'Max hold' on RESPONSE switch. The display will only display the highest reading in the mode.

Results and Inference:

EXPERIMENT 9

Estimation of Species Abundance of Plants

Introduction

In nature, different kinds of organisms grow in association with each other. A group of several species (plants and / or animals) living together with mutual tolerance and beneficial interactions in natural ecosystem is known as a community. In a community, organisms share the same habitat growing in an uniform environment. Each community is characterized by its species diversity, growth forms and structure dominance, survival trend *etc.* Plants growing together have mutual relationship among themselves and with environment. Such group of plants in one area forms a stand. Several similar stands represent a community. It is part of ecological system in which, transformation, accumulation and flow of energy are involved. The functioning of this system is intimately related with the components of the community. The components vary in quantity as well as in quality and impart a structure to the community.

Aim

To study the vegetation in an area by line transect method and to determine the frequency of individual species.

Requirements

Measuring tape, graph sheet *etc.*

Procedure

- Run the measuring tape across the vegetation
- Note down the species touching the tape in alternate segments of suitable length.
- A number of transect can be laid down at random in the field at different sites. Thus, in the case, one meter segment is the unit of study. If any plant species is touching the segment, the numerical strength of that species in that sampling unit will be three individuals. This value may be written against the respective species below that sampling unit.

Observations

Name of plants	No. of sampling unit										Total No. individual plants
	1	2	3	4	5	6	7	8	9	10	
A											
B											
C											
D											
E											
F											
G											
H											
I											
J											

Studying the Vegetation by Point Frame Method

Aim

To study the vegetation by point frame method and determining the frequency of each species present.

Requirements

Point frame apparatus, graph sheet *etc.*

Procedure

- The apparatus with 10 pins put at a place is one sampling unit. Put the apparatus in random at a number of places (20 or more) in the field.
- Note down each time the various species hit by one or more of the 10 pins and thus, pin is one sampling unit.
- Distribute the various frequencies among five frequency classes and find out the % value in each frequency class.

Quantification of Species Abundance

(i) ***Frequency:*** It is number of sampling unit (as %) in which a particular species occurs.

$$\text{Frequency }(\%) = \frac{\text{No. of sampling units in which the species occurred}}{\text{Total No. of sampling units studied}}$$

After determining the percentage frequency of each species, various species are distributed among Raunkier's five frequency classes depending upon their frequency values.

Frequency %	Frequency class
0 to 20	A
21 to 40	B
41 to 60	C
61 to 80	D
81 to 100	E

Calculations

Name of the plant	Frequency (%)	Density	Abundance	Relative Frequency	Relative Density	Relative Abundance	IVI
A							
B							
C							
D							
E							
F							
G							
H							
I							
J							

(ii) ***Density*:** It represents the numerical strength of a species in the community. The number of individuals of the species in any unit area is its density. Density gives an idea of competition.

$$\text{Density} = \frac{\text{Total No. of individuals of the species in all the sampling units}}{\text{Total No. of sampling units studied}}$$

The value obtained is then expressed as number of individuals per unit area.

(iii) ***Abundance*:** This is the number of individuals of any species per sampling unit of occurrence.

$$\text{Abundance} = \frac{\text{Total No. of individuals of species in all the sampling units}}{\text{No. of sampling units in which the species occurred}}$$

(iv) **Relative density**

$$\text{Relative density} = \frac{\text{Density of the species}}{\text{Total density of all the species}} \times 100$$

(v) **Relative frequency**

$$\text{Relative frequency} = \frac{\text{Frequency of the species}}{\text{frequency of all the species}} \times 100$$

(vi) **Relative abundance**

$$\text{Relative abundance} = \frac{\text{Abundance of the species}}{\text{Totalabundance of all the species}} \times 100$$

(vii) Important Value Index (IVI)

IVI = Relative density + Relative Abundance + Relative frequency

Results and Inference:

EXPERIMENT 10

Estimation of Non-Respirable Dust in Air by Using Dust Sampler

Introduction

Troposphere is regarded as the locus of most weather phenomena which effect different eco systems of biosphere. Therefore, the quality of air in this lower 11 km is very important. For studying the quality of air, first step is to draw representative sample for analysis. Physical factors related to air are measured in the field using special monitoring instruments. Chemical properties are measured in two ways *i.e.,* measurement of the samples collected at the spot and continuous monitoring in that spot. The main pollutants in air are suspended particulate matter, aerosols, toxic gases *etc.*

Suspended Particulate Matter

The particulate matter in air may occur as solid, liquid and both. The common solid forms are dust, fumes and smoke while common liquid forms are fog and mist. Particles larger than a molecule but small enough to remain dispersed in air are called aerosols. The particulate matter in air is a variable component and is introduced through natural phenomena like wind, volcanic eruptions, pollen and spores, decomposition of organic matter *etc.,* or through human activities like industrial processes, mining, burning of fuel *etc.* Air borne particles are considered to be a nuisance to industries requiring clean and aseptic atmosphere like drug and food industry. They may cause diseases like allergic asthma, bronchitis, and even fibrosis of lungs. Dust particles when deposited on the photosynthetic surfaces effect the photosynthesis, growth and yield of agricultural crops. Certain trees are found to be good dust collectors rendering the air clean.

Different methods like gravitational method, impaction method, electrostatic precipitation method and filtration method are in vogue to assess suspended particulate matter (SPM) in the air. Broadly particulate matter is categorized into two sizes: >10 microns (non-respirable SPM) and < 10 microns (respirable SPM).

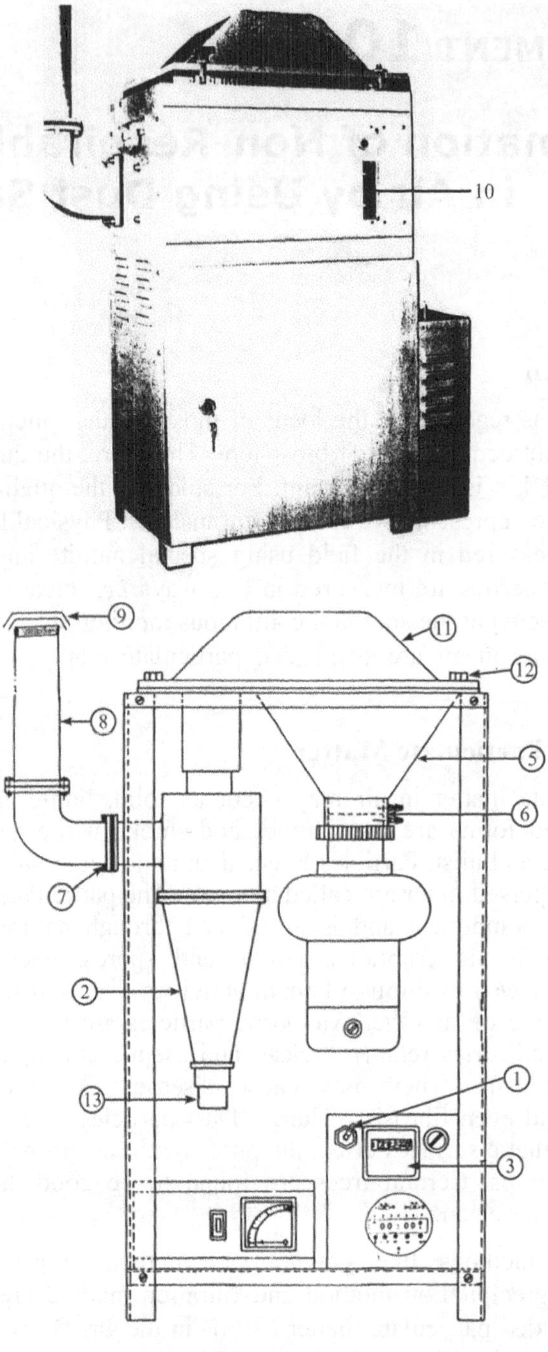

Layout of Main parts of APM 460

Gravitational method

This method can be used to evaluate the dust fall within a city or an industrial shed, and usually it accounts for particles of 1 micron or larger size. Put the clean glass jars of known open area in the atmosphere where dust fall is to be estimated. After a sufficient gap of time (some hours or days) collect the dust settled in each jar and weigh it. Take an average weight of dust fall to be expressed as weight of dust per unit area per unit time.

Filtration method (high volume sampling)

Pass a large known volume of air through a pre-weighed glass fibre filter (Whatman GF/C) and then measure the increase in the weight of filter due to trapped particles. Calculate the particulate matter per unit volume of air. By this method particles as small as 0.05 microns can be measured.

Estimation of Non-respirable Suspended Particulate Matter

The pollutants in air has been classified as natural contaminants – natural fog, pollen grains, bacteria and products of volcanic eruption. Size of these particles is greater than 10 microns. Mostly these particles are referred to as the non respirable dust. Particulate matter is classified into different categories based on the size of particles:

Dust: dust is made up of solid particles. They are mainly produced by crushing and grinding of inorganic and organic materials. Their size vary from 1 - 200 μ.

Mists: this refers to dispersion of liquid particles of large size. The size varies from 40-500 μ.

Fog: fog refers to visible aerosols in which dispersed phase is liquid. The size varies from 1-40 μ.

Fumes: These are solid particles generated by condensation from the gaseous state.

Aim

To estimate the amount of non-respirable suspended particulate matter in the air using high volume sampler.

Apparatus

Respirable dust sampler APM 460, balance

Observations

Empty weight of sampling bottle = W_1 gms

Weight of sampling bottle after the after the sampling time = W_2 gms

Wt of dust collected = $(W_2 - W_1)$ gms

Initial flow rate of air = Q_1 (m^3/min)

Finial flow rate of air = Q_2 (m^3/min)

Sampling time in minutes = T

Calculations

Total volume of air sampled in m^3

$$V = \frac{(Q_1 + Q_2)}{2} \times T$$

Mass concentration of suspended particulates in µg $m^3 = \frac{(W_2 - W_1)}{V} \times 10^6$

Principle

Ambient air laden with suspended particulates enters the system through the inlet pipe. As the air passes through the cyclone, coarse non-respirable dust is separated from the air stream by centrifugal forces acting on the solid particles. These separated particulates fall through the cyclone's conical hopper and collect in the sampling bottle fitted at its bottom.

Procedure

- The air inlet pipe (8) is attached to the cyclone inlet by four socket head cap screws (7).
- Mount and screw the inlet cover cap (9) on the top of the inlet pipe.
- The manometer assembly (10) is provided to accurately measure the pressure drop across the orifice plate built into the filter adaptor and its scale is graduated to read directly the flow rate of air in m^3/minute.
- Fill the manometer with distilled water with the help of a syringe to the zero mark. Then replace the filling plug screw and tighten it in place.
- Remove the dust collection bottle (4) at the bottom of the cyclone (2).
- Use a small paint brush to clean any dust residues at the bottom hole of the cyclone body.
- Replace a clean pre-weighed dust collection bottle and push it upwards until it rests firmly against the bottom seal ring.
- The weight of the sampling bottle is noted prior to sampling.
- Set the on-off timer (3) to start the sampling for the prescribed time (24 hr) recording the starting time. After 5 minute, note down the flow rate.
- Turn switch (1) to ON position and RUN the motor.
- At the end of sampling period, record the length of sampling period and flow rate.
- At the end of sampling period, note down the weight of the dust collection bottle.
- The difference in weight is non-respirable dust.

Precautions

1. The manometer scale is not linear and it is important to carefully zero the level of the liquid column prior to use without air bubbles.
2. Ensure to keep clean sampling bottle initially.

Results and Inference:

EXPERIMENT 11

Estimation of Respirable Dust in Air by Using Dust Sampler

Introduction

All microorganisms responsible for causing respiratory, eye and skin diseases, various allergins, fibrous materials, heavy metals, metallic fumes and even many organic carcinogens are present in the air in the form of suspended particles. Health effects are caused primarily by respirable particulates in the size range of 0.5 to 10 microns. Hence, suspended particulate matter (SPM) in air has been considered a 'criteria parameter' all over the world to indicate air quality. Smoke generally consists of finely divided particles of size 0.2-0.01μ produced by incomplete combustion. Aerosols vary in size from 0.01 μ to 10 μ, refer to the dispersion of solid or liquid particles in gaseous media such as dust smoke or mist.

Aim

To estimate the amount of respirable dust in the air using high volume air sampler.

Apparatus

Respirable dust sampler APM 460, balance, filter paper, desiccator.

Principle

Ambient air laden with suspended particulates enters the system through the inlet pipe. As the air passes through the cyclone, non-respirable dust is separated from the air stream by centrifugal forces acting on the solid particles and is collected separately in a sampling bottle. The fine dust forming the respirable fraction of the suspended particulate matter passes through the cyclone and is carried by the air stream to the filter paper clamped between the top cover and filter adaptor assembly. The respirable dust is retained by the filter and the carrier air is exhausted from the system through the blower.

Observations

Weight of filter paper before fixing it in the dust sampler = W_1 gms

Weight of the filter paper after the after the sampling time = W_2 gms

Weight of dust collected = $(W_2 - W_1)$ gms

Initial flow rate of air = Q_1 (m^3/min)

Finial flow rate of air = Q_2 (m^3/min)

Sampling time in minutes = T

Calculations

Total volume of air sampled in m^3

$$V = \frac{(Q_1 + Q_2)}{2} \times T$$

Mass concentration of suspended particulates in µg $m^3 = \frac{(W_2 - W_1)}{V} \times 10^6$

Procedure

- The air inlet pipe (8) is attached to the cyclone inlet by four socket head cap screws (7) (parts of the dust sampler are marked in page 58).
- Mount and screw the inlet cover cap (9) on the top of the inlet pipe.
- The manometer assembly (10) is provided to accurately measure the pressure drop across the orifice plate (6) built into the filter adaptor (5) and its scale is graduated to read directly the flow rate of air in m^3/minute.
- Fill the manometer with distilled water with the help of a syringe to the zero mark. Then replace the filling plug screw and tighten it in place.
- Check the fibre glass filter for pin holes, particles or other imperfections. Filters with visible imperfections should not be used.
- Equilibrate the filter in the dessicator for 24 hrs and weigh to the nearest milligram.
- Record the weight and note it as W_I (do not fold or bend the filter before collection of sample)
- Open the shelter (11) of the high volume sampler, loosen the wing nuts (12) and remove the face plate from filter holder.
- Install a pre-weighed glass fiber filter in position.
- Close the roof of the shelter
- Set the on-off timer to start the sampling for the prescribed time (24 hr) recording the starting time. After 5 minutes note down the flow rate.
- Turn switch (1) to ON position and RUN the motor.
- At the end of sampling period, record the length of sampling period and flow rate.
- Remove the filter paper and record its final weight as W_2

Precautions

1. The manometer scale is not linear and it is important to carefully zero the level of the liquid column prior to use without air bubbles.
2. Ensure to keep clean sampling bottle initially.
3. Filter paper should be without even pin holes, should be dry, numbered and weighed accurately.

Results and Inference:

EXPERIMENT 12

Study of Transpiration and Water Balance in Plants

Introduction

Water balance studies aid in characterization of fundamental physiological responses of plants to drought stress or to identify genetic variability in the genotypes. The identified species could be used either in breeding programmes or in further phenotyping studies.

Aim

To estimate the water requirement of given genotypes / crops and arrive at a balance sheet for the dry matter produced

Principle

Gravimetric approach makes it possible to maintain precise level of water requirement or stress at whole plant level. Plant responses to water deficits are often measured under green house or other controlled environmental conditions.

Water stress can be imposed more slowly akin to the natural environment if total plant available water is increased either by using large containers. In such studies the rate at which water stress develops or growth increase depends on the environmental conditions (radiation load, air temperature, humidity) which may vary depending on the water use rates of individual plants. A more consistent treatment that synchronizes well with the experimental units or pots can be achieved by using smaller pots by determining water loss from each pot gravimetrically on a regular basis and replacing part of the transpired water to control the rate of soil dry down. The approach is referred to as gravimetric approach for drought induction studies or assessment of genetic variability and their characterization

For example the amount of water required to maintain 100% FC = x ml

The amount of water required to maintain 60% FC

$$= 60\% \times x \text{ ml}/ 100\% = \ldots \text{ ml}$$

Calculations

Pot No.	Date	Amount of water added to bring to 60% FC (ml)	Weight of the plant (g)	Remarks
1				
2				
3				
4				
5				

Materials

Plastic pots, garden soil (soil: sand: manure in the ratio of 2:1:1), mobile weighing device, seed or plant material

Procedure

- Take the empty pot and note down the weight.
- Fill the pots with air dried soil
- Weigh the pot along with soil and deduct the empty pot weight to obtain the dry soil weight
- Flood the pot with water to saturate soil and leave it overnight to reach field capacity (FC)
- Take the pot weight along with wet soil and deduct the empty pot weight to get the wet soil weight. The dry soil weight is subtracted from the wet soil weight to get the amount of water required to maintain 100% FC
- Sow the seeds of the crop. Two seedlings may be maintained in each pot and watered regularly to maintain moisture level at 100% FC in a poly house till six leaf stage.
- Then maintain the crop at 60% FC.
- Take continuous observations at weekly intervals from six leaf stage. Record the amount of water added to maintain 60% FC *i.e.,* mild stress. At each observation interval pull out the plant and take the dry weight of the entire plant or its component parts. Equate the amount of water added and the dry weight increase to know the water balance in plants

Discussion

Variation among the genotypes or between crop plants for water requirement could be quantified over a period of time. The genotype which takes little amount of water and puts forth growth or reaches a particular growth stage is considered as a water saver or otherwise water spender. Based on the computation of water requirement and dry matter produced, water balance is arrived at for a genotype. Maintenance of dequate amount of plants / pots would aid in reducing the error and arriving at a water balance sheet for the particular genotype under consideration.

Results and Inference

EXPERIMENT 13

Assessment of Chlorophyll Content in Plants

Introduction

Chlorophyll is the essential component for photosynthesis, and occur in chloroplasts as green colored pigment. They are bound loosely to proteins but are readily extracted in organic solvents such as acetone or ether. Chemically, each chlorophyll molecule contains a prophyrin (tetrapyrole) nucleus with a chelated magnesium atom at the centre and a long-chain hydrocarbon (phytyl) side chain attached through a carboxylic acid group. There are at least five types. Chlorophyll c, d and e are only found in algae and in certain bacteria. There are two methods to estimate chlorophyll content of plants namely Destructive method and Non-destructive method.

Destructive method

Aim

Estimation of chlorophyll content in leaves (normal vs. stressed) using acetone.

Apparatus

Glass mortar and pestle, 50 ml volumetric flask, spectro photometer

Reagents

Diluted analytical grade acetone (80 %) (prechilled).

Observations

Absorbance at specific wave lengths = A
Final volume of chlorophyll extract with 80% acetone made up = V = 50 ml
Fresh weight of effected leaf taken for extraction = W gm

Calculations

$$\text{Chlorophyll - a (mg/g of tissue)} = [12.7A_{663} - 2.69A_{645}] \times \left[\frac{V}{1000 \times W}\right]$$

$$\text{Chlorophyll - b (mg/g of tissue)} = [22.9A_{645} - 4.68A_{663}] \times \left[\frac{V}{1000 \times W}\right]$$

$$\text{Chlorophyll - total (mg/g of tissue)} = [A_{652} \times 1000/34.5] \times \left[\frac{V}{1000 \times W}\right]$$

Principle

Different chlorophylls absorb light energy differently and each type of it has got its own absorption peak. Chlorophyll is extracted in 80 % acetone and the absorption is read in a spectrophotometer at 663 nm and 645 nm. Using the absorption coefficient, the amount of chlorophyll is calculated.

Procedure

- Weigh each 1 g of finely cut and well mixed representative sample of leaf into a clean glass mortar separately. Avoid mid rib.
- Grind the tissue with a pestle to a fine pulp with the addition of pinch of $CaCO_3$ and 15 ml of 80% acetone.
- Filter and transfer the filtrate into a 50 ml volumetric flask.
- Grind the residue with 10 ml of 80% acetone, filter and transfer the filtrate to the same volumetric flask.
- Wash the mortar and pestle thoroughly with 80% acetone and collect the clear washings in the same volumetric flask.
- Make up the volume to 50 ml with 80% acetone.
- Read the absorbance of the solution at 645, 652 and 663 nm using spectrophotometer against the blank (80% acetone).

Results and Inference

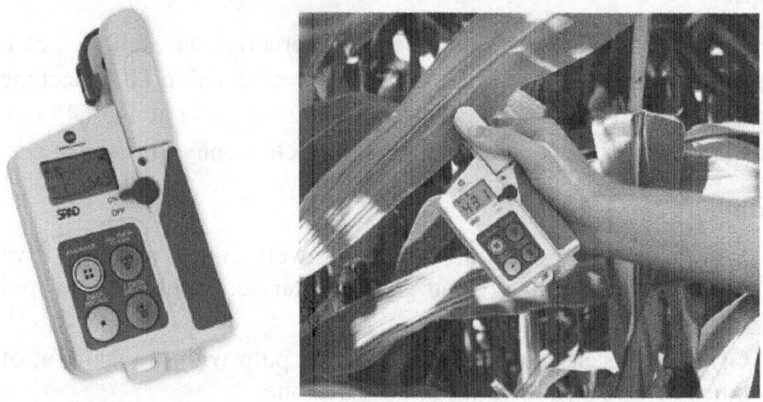

SPAD Meter

Observations

S No.	Particulars of sample	SPAD units
1		
2		
3		
5		
6		
7		

Non-destructive method

Aim

Estimation of chlorophyll content in leaves (normal vs. stressed) using SPAD meter.

Principle

The SPAD-502 determines the relative amount of chlorophyll present by measuring the absorbance of the leaf in two wavelength regions. The chlorophyll has absorbance peaks in the blue (400-500 nm) and red (600-700 nm) regions, with no transmittance in the near-infrared region. To take advantage of this characteristic of chlorophyll, the SPAD-502 measures the absorbance of the leaf in the red and near-infrared regions. Using these two transmittances, the meter calculates numerical SPAD value which is proportional to the amount of chlorophyll present in the leaf.

Equipment: SPAD meter

Procedure

- The SPAD-502 can be easily used to take measurements in the field. The measuring area is only 2 mm × 3 mm, allowing small leaves to be measured, and sample may be up to 1.2 mm thick.
- Perform calibration.
- Insert the sample to be measured into the sample slot of the measuring head.
- If measurements are on a leaf that has many fine veins, take several measurements and average them for best results.
- Press on the finger rest to close the measuring head. Hold it closed until a beep sounds and the measured value appears in the display. The measurement will automatically be stored in memory.

Precautions

1. Do not use the chlorophyll meter when the plant is under stress because the readings will not be accurate.
2. Avoid collecting readings from areas of the field that are not well drained or from wet leaves because moisture can distort the readings.
3. Avoid taking readings from diseased field.
4. On the fields receiving manure applications, use the chlorophyll meter in conjunction with nitrogen testing of 3 foot-deep soil samples.
5. Don't leave the meter in direct sunlight because extreme temperature changes can cause meter readings to fluctuate.

Results and Inference

EXPERIMENT 14

Visit to *In situ* or *Ex situ* Conservation Centre / Social Service Organisation / Environmental Education Centre

'Biological diversity' or biodiversity is a part of nature which includes the differences in genes among the individuals of a species; the variety and richness of all the plant and animal species at different scales in space - locally, in a region, in the country and the world; and the types of ecosystems, both terrestrial and aquatic, within a defined area. "Biodiversity" was coined as a contraction of a "biological diversity" in 1985. The rapid loss of species, we are seeing today, is estimated to be between 1000 and 10,000 times higher than the natural extinction.

In general terms, population growth and our consumption are the reasons for this enormous loss. Specifically habitat destruction and wildlife trade are the major causes for population decline in species. The economic value of the reservoir of genetic traits present in wild varieties and traditionally grown land races is extremely important in improving crop performance. Important crops, such as the potato and coffee, are often derived from only a few genetic strains. Improvement in crop plants over the last 250 years have been largely due to harnessing the genetic diversity present in wild and domestic crop plants. Interbreeding crop strains with different beneficial traits has resulted in more than doubling crop production in the last 50 years as a result of the Green Revolution.

Conservation of Biodiversity

The three goals of conservation Framework are:

1. Contribution to global efforts for conservation.
2. Prevention of species and ecosystems from becoming at risk.
3. Maintenance of diversity of native species and ecosystems.

There are two main ways to conserve biodiversity – *in situ* (with in the natural habitat) and *ex situ* (out of natural habitat) conservation.

***In situ* conservation** means "on-site conservation". It is the process of protecting an endangered plant or animal species within its natural habitat, either by protecting or cleaning up of the field, or by defending the species from predators. This term refers also to the conservation of genetic resources in natural populations of plant or animal species, such as forest in natural populations of tree species, and is increasingly being applied to conservation of agricultural biodiversity in agro--systems by farmers, especially those using unconventional farming practices. One benefit to *in situ* conservation is that it maintains recovering populations in the surrounding where they have developed their distinctive properties. Another is that this strategy helps to ensure the ongoing processes of evolution and adaptation within their environments. As a last resort *ex*--situ conservation may be used on some or all of the population, when *in-situ* conservation is too difficult or impossible.

Examples: National parks and Sanctuaries

***Ex situ* conservation** means literally "off-site conservation". It is the process of protecting an endangered species of plant or animal by removing part of the population from a threatened habitat and placing it in a new location which may be a wild area or within the care of humans. Zoos and botanical gardens are the most conventional methods of *ex situ* conservation, all of which house whole, protected specimens for breeding and reintroduction into the wild when necessary and possible. These facilities provide not only housing and care for specimens of endangered species, but also have an educational value. They inform the public of the threatened status of endangered species and of those factors which cause the threat, with the hope of creating public interest in stopping and reversing those factors which jeopardize a species' survival in the first place annually. Endangered plants may also be preserved in part through seed banks or germ plasm banks. The term seed bank sometimes refers to a cryogenic laboratory facility in which the seeds of certain species can be preserved for up to a century or more without loosing their fertility. It can also be used to refer to a special type of arboretum where seeds are harvested and the crop is rotated. For plants that cannot be preserved in seed banks, the only other option for preserving germ plasm is *in vitro* storage, where cuttings of plants are kept under strict conditions in glass tubes and vessels.

Endangered animal species are preserved using similar techniques. The genetic information needed in the future to reproduce endangered animal species can be preserved in gene banks, which consist of cryogenic facilities used to store species that was thought to be extinct.

Drawbacks

Ex situ conservation, while helpful in man's efforts to sustain and protect our environment, is rarely enough to save species from extinction. It is to be used as a last resort or as a supplement to *in situ* conservation because it cannot recreate the habitat as a whole: the entire genetic variation of a species, its symbiotic counterparts, or those elements which, over time, might help a species adapt to its changing surroundings. Instead, *ex situ* conservation removes the species from its natural ecological contexts, preserving it under semi-isolated conditions whereby natural evolution and adaptation processes are either temporarily halted or altered by introducing the specimen to an unnatural habitat. In the case of cryogenic storage methods, the preserved specimen's adaptation processes are frozen altogether. The downside to this is that, when re-released, the species may lack the genetic adaptations and mutations which would allow it to thrive in its ever-changing natural habitat. Furthermore, *ex situ* conservation techniques are often costly, with cryogenic storage being economically infeasible in most cases since species stored in this manner cannot provide a profit but instead slowly drain the financial resources of the government or organization determined to operate them. Seed banks are ineffective for certain plant genera with recalcitrant seeds that do not remain fertile for long periods of time. Diseases and pests foreign to the species, to which the species has no natural defense, may also cripple crops of protected plants in *ex situ* plantations and in animals living in *ex situ* breeding grounds. These factors, combined with the specific environmental needs of many species, some of which are nearly impossible to recreate by man, make *ex situ* conservation impossible for a great number.

Experiment

Aim:

Visit to *In situ* or *Ex situ* conservation centre/ Social Service Organization / Environmental Education Centre to bring awareness on conservation of biodiversity

Observations:

Write a brief note on the centre you have visited

EXPERIMENT 15

Information and Communication Technology in Environmental Science

Environmental concerns have been addressed at a rapid pace in the last few years due to the sudden growth of information technology. Information technology has spread the knowledge rapidly, accurately into world networks. Computers around us have turned the world around and made it into a global village.

Information and communication technologies (ICTs) can further improve environmental performance and address climate change issues. Smarter and cleaner environmental and economic strategies can tackle the challenge of global warming and contribute to "green growth" and clean innovation in the economic crisis and recovery. ICTs and the Internet have key roles in increasing energy efficiency, reducing energy use and managing scarce resources. Smart ICT applications and the internet can enable energy efficiency improvements in areas as diverse as buildings, transport and logistics, electricity generation, distribution and consumption. Sensor-based broadband applications can foster effective responses to environmental change as well as improving efficiency of current systems. As products and services become "digital", online delivery can also reduce environmental impacts across all sectors of the economy. At the same time, rising energy demands of some ICT infrastructures need to be addressed to lower the environmental impact of a rapidly widening range of ICT products and applications products. The ICT sector needs to mitigate its own environmental impact through better life-cycle audits of ICT products and production processes, and R&D and innovation to improve product design.

Information and communication technologies (ICTs) are crucial in reducing poverty, improving access to health and education services and creating new sources of income and employment for the poor. But there are substantial discrepancies in access to ICTs between, but also within, countries, depending on key factors such as gender, rural coverage, skills and educational levels.

Some of the local specific issues concerning one and all can become a big list. Some of them can be accessed and information about them can be obtained at the following **Uniform Resource Locator** (URL)

1. **Approved Package of Practices for cotton: Andhra Pradesh**

   http://cicr.nic.in/pop/ap.pdf

   The URL covers recommended Cultivars, prominent cultivars in cultivation, Soil/Areas, Land preparation, Seed and Planting method and time, Seed treatment, Inter cropping, Cropping systems, Fertilizers recommended for different regions of Andhra Pradesh, Micronutrients Deficiencies, Inter cultivation and other Management Practices, Irrigation, Pest Management, Integrated pest management in cotton, Disease Management, Harvesting and Post Harvesting Technology

2. **Disaster management**

   http://en.wikipedia.org/wiki/Wikipedia:WikiProject_Disaster_management

   Site covers Disasters, *viz.,* Natural disasters, Severe weather, Man-made disaster. Information covered includes **Emergencies,** International development, Fire Services, Law enforcement; **Hazards,** Earthquakes; **Environment**, Meteorology, Tropical cyclones, Terrorism and counter-terrorism. Environment further includes topics like Climate change & Global warming, Conservation movement, Environmentalism, Environmental Science, Renewable energy, Sustainability, Waste & Waste management

3. **Environment of India**

   http://en.wikipedia.org/wiki/Category:Environment_of_India

   Information is provided on the following topics: Lights Out, Appiko movement, Drought in India, Effects of global warming on India, Energising India, Environmental policy of the Government of India, Forestry in India, Indian natural history, Ministry of Environment and Forests (India), Natural disasters in India, Red rain in Kerala, Chipko movement

[illegible] issues concern [illegible] and all can be geographic[illegible]. Some of them can be accessed and information about them can be obtained at the following [illegible] Resource Locator (URL):

1. Approved Package of Practices for cotton, Andhra Pradesh

[illegible]

[illegible]

2. [illegible]

[illegible]

[illegible]

3. Government of India

[illegible]

[illegible]

4. **Indigenous ecological knowledge, biodiversity and sustainable development in the central Himalayas**

   http://www.tropecol.com/pdf/open/PDF_44_1/44110.pdf

   Information is provided on Traditional agriculture and emerging changes, Traditional water management and changes therein, Soil loss from different crop fields and terrace slope in the Pranmati watershed of the central Himalayas, Soil fertility recovery and carbon sequestration, Incremental improvement in traditional agroforestry systems.

   Other international frameworks include the United Nations Statistics Division (UNSD) Framework for the Development of Environment Statistics, published in 1984. A set of indicators is based on the Framework and covers economic, social and environment issues. The UN Commission on Sustainable Development list of CSD13 indicators includes economic, social and environmental themes, in the context of sustainable development. CSD environment indicators include Climate change, air quality, land use and degradation, forest cover, freshwater availability and quality and biodiversity.

   World Wide Fund for Nature (WWF). - mission is "to stop the degradation of the planets natural environment and to build a future in which humans live in harmony with nature…" It started work with ICT in 2000 and works with other organizations, including the WEF.

Practical exercise

Sudents to retrieve information from the URL's and submit a small project for record and further evaluation

EXPERIMENT 16

Visit to a Local Polluted Site – Observation and Remedial Measures

Pollution is the effect of undesirable changes in our surroundings that have harmful effects on plants, animals and human beings. Pollutants include solid, liquid or gaseous substances present in greater than natural abundance produced due to human activity, which have a detrimental effect on our environment. Polluted sites include urban, rural, agriculture and industrial areas.

Pollution can affect

1. Air (smoke, gases)
2. Water (urban sewage, industrial chemical effluents, agricultural pesticides and fertilizers)
3. Soil (chemicals, solid waste from industry and urban areas)
4. Biodiversity (effects on plant and animal life)

Pollution occurs when only short-term economic gains are made at the cost of long-term ecological benefits for humanity. During the last few decades we have contaminated our air, water and land on which life itself depends with a variety of waste products.

Aim

To study the cause and effects of pollution at the site

Methodology

Certain key questions related to the polluted site are given below. Explore the site to answer the questions about the area you have visited

- What is the site?
- Rural – agricultural area, polluted water body, polluted industrial area
  Urban – solid waste management site, polluted industrial area

What do you observe at the polluted site?

Solid waste- garbage dump, polluted water at a river or lake, gaseous effluents or smoke coming out of an industry area, etc

- Explore the reasons for pollution. Observe and document the components in the garbage/the polluted water body/industrial chimneys.
- Observe the area and list the waste that is seen in the polluted site.
- Categorize the wastes at the site. For example, in garbage dumping site it can be categorized into three types.
    - Degradable wastes are those which are easily decomposed by microorganisms. These include food wastes, plant material, animal carcasses *etc.*
    - Non-degradable wastes are those which are not easily decomposed *e.g.,* plastic, glass.
    - Toxic wastes are those that are poisonous and cause long term effects *e.g.* several chemicals, paints, sprays.

Findings

- What are the effects of the pollutant?
- What actions can you take to get pollution reduced?

General observations

The following aspects need to be observed and documented:

- The type of land or water use in the polluted area, its geographical characteristics, who uses the area, who owns it.
- Map the area to be studied.
- Identifying what is being polluted – air, water, soil; the cause(s) of pollution and the polluting agent(s)
- Assess the extent of pollution- severe / moderate/ slight / nil, to: the air, water, soil, biodiversity.
- Assess from literature, the health aspects associated with the pollutant.
- Ask local residents about its effects on their lives.
- Make a report of the above findings.

APPENDIX - I

List of Glasswares

1. Beakers – 1000 ml
2. Beakers – 100 ml
3. Beakers – 500 ml
4. BOD bottles
5. Burette with stand
6. China dish
7. COD reflux Unit
8. Conical flasks – 100 ml
9. Conical flasks – 250 ml
10. Desiccator
11. Glass mortar and pestle
12. Glass or Plastic bottles with tightly fitting screw cap
13. Glass rod
14. Measuring tape
15. Pipette 10 ml
16. Pipette 50 ml
17. Plastic pots
18. Porcelain dish

APPENDIX – II

List of Chemicals

1. Ammonium chloride
2. Ammonium hydroxide
3. Calcium carbonate
4. Calcium chloride
5. Conc. Sulphuric acid (AR)
6. Conc. Hydrochloric Acid
7. DTPA(AR)
8. EDTA salt (AR)
9. Eriochrome Black T
10. Ethanol
11. Ferrous ammonium sulphate (AR)
12. Formaldehyde
13. Manganous sulphate
14. Mercuric Sulphate ($HgSo_4$)
15. Methyl Orange
16. Murexide
17. Nickel standard solution (AR)
18. Phenonthroline
19. Potassium dichromate (AR)
20. Potassium hydroxide (AR)
21. Potassium iodide
22. Potassium sulphate
23. Silver Sulphate
24. Sodium hydroxide (AR)
25. Sodium thiosulphate(AR)
26. Starch
27. Standard solutions for Cr, Co, Ni, Cd & Pb
28. Triethanol amine

APPENDIX – III

List of Equipment

1. Atomic Absorption spectrophotometer
2. COD digestion unit.
3. Dust sampler
4. Electronic balance
5. Hot water bath
6. Sound level meter
7. SPAD meter
8. Spectrophometer

References

1. Lenore. S. Clesceri, Arnold E.Greenbarg and Andrew D.Eaton, *Standard Methods for the Examination of Water and Waste water 20th Edition*, American Public Health Association, APHA, 1015 15th Street, NW, Washington, DC 2005.

2. Neemima Rajvaidya, Dilip Kumar Markandey, *Environmental Analysis and Instrumentation* A.P.H.P. Publishing Corporation, 5, Ansari Road, Darya Ganj, New Delhi – 110 002.

3. Tandon HLS *Methods of Analysis of Soils, Plants, Waters and Fertilisers*, published by Wadha International, B-193, Okhla Phase-I, New Delhi – 110020.